SINGING THROUGH MY
WOLF BONES

SINGING THROUGH MY WOLF BONES

Poems of Reclamation & Healing

TIANNA G. HANSEN

Wolf Rose Press

Contents

Wolf Rose Press
an imprint
Birdsboro, PA

Second Printing, July 2022

Hardcover ISBN 978-1-952050-04-6
Paperback ISBN 978-1-952050-99-2
E-book ISBN 978-1-952050-98-5

creativetianna.com/books

for all the wild (wolf) women
who wear their fur like armor

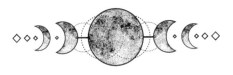

Infinite gratitude to:
my human pack for accepting me in wolf form;
and to my husband, for still loving me when I began to howl.

Dedicated with special love to
all my sisters of flesh, fur, bone & blood…
*especially dear **Maya**, whose healing helps so many,*
*& **to our mother**, for raising us both since birth.*

* * *

"Let the waters settle
and you will see
the moon and the stars
mirrored in your own being."

~Rumi

Author's Note

Lycanthropy: How it Begins

There exists within each of us a Dual nature ~ when we learn to embrace and connect with our Shadow, we discover our power. The Wild & Tame, Dark & Light, Feminine & Masculine. . . the Balance within each of us that makes us not one or the other, but equal. Once we learn to embrace this Duality, we learn how to be Freely ourSelf, an extension of the Universe. We begin to heal from all that still causes us pain (either realized or yet unknown); we harness our power within, through courage, vulnerability, and living with a Whole Heart. We learn how to Soar.

.:.

Wolves embody this Duality in infinite ways. Not only are they thought of (and vilified by pop culture and politics), as wild creatures who are dangerous and violent (and though they can be this way), their gentler, vital nature is often not shown or discussed by the media. Many of the poems in this book are in conversation with the common terms of phrase we've come to associate with the wolf, challenging our own societal thinking and conditioning while asking the reader to take a step further, into a deeper meditation on the Dual strength and softness of the wolf.

.:.

This collection is as much about lycanthropy as identity—

growing into mySelf and embracing Nature in all its beauty; becoming part of the world around me while also discovering my inner power. *Writing this, something inside broke free.*

Wolves have always fascinated me, but I never planned for them to become an emblem of my healing. I wrote the first twenty wolf-themed poems over a week's time in what felt like a feverish state. I stayed up late writing, half-conscious; insatiable.

.·.

As if bitten by a wolf, undergoing my own transformation, this collection was born. Each poem a howl, bursting from my throat onto the page. Each poem a new inner discovery, a rebirth and reclamation. The Wolf's expression of freedom, their ability to race through the woods, howl at the moon, discard vulnerable flesh for a fiercer nature. . . (A word I love is '*eleutheromania*': an intense and irresistible desire for freedom).

Wolves lead by instinct and senses alone; their sight, sound, taste, touch, and smell are powerful ~ and they are acutely, keenly aware of all who exist and step foot within their territory. SURVIVAL is always at the forefront of a wolf's mind and purpose; they are wild creatures tuned into the world around them; without questioning who or *why* they are.

.·.

This book has morphed over the course of four years, written throughout a time when I felt untethered from life, love and identity, working to reclaim myself and my desires. Working to channel the inner wolf I didn't yet know would come out full-force, but also working to soften. To live warm and human, vulnerable and embracing my fears and emotions. Living with this Duality inside; the will to be both fierce and gentle. Leading with compassion as I entered the shadowy forest of the mind to write my way back out again.

In a rush, the poetry flowed. I wrote by pure instinct, researched avidly, read voraciously (as I love to do). I pulled inspiration and influence from folklore, the occult, and modern culture – films, books and music (a list of some inspirations can be found in the back). I studied werewolf literature, occult rituals, tales passed down for centuries, and all the ways that (were)wolves have infiltrated our modern culture ~ from ancient legends until today.

.:.

This poetry is very much the essence of my Wild Woman coming out to howl at the moon, rampaging through the forest in great bounds and leaps. As Clarissa Pinkola Estés, PhD writes in *Women Who Run With the Wolves*, "**[The Wild Woman] comes to us through sound as well; through music which vibrates the sternum, excites the heart; it comes through the drum, the whistle, the call, and the cry. It comes through the written and the spoken word; sometimes a word, a sentence or a poem or a story, is so resonant, so right, it causes us to remember, at least for an instant, what substance we are really made from, and where is our true home.**"

Writing this collection resonated with me like coming home. As I wrote and channeled the wolf, I recognized and embraced the Wild Woman inside me. Both soft and passionate; bold and delicate.

.:.

Thank you, dear reader, for joining me on this journey. I hope as you read, you may find pieces of yourself inside these writings; or at the very least, rejoice in the freedom I found myself, while writing them.

Stay Wild.

~ *Tianna*

Prelude: Longing

"We all have a longing for the wild."
~Clarissa Pinkola Estés

ODE TO THE WANDERING ONE

~ for Nikai

you hang back from the others, great
mysteries hidden in your eyes. white
coat like an apparition appearing
through the trees. you are hesitant,
shy and gentle. you wait for a slice
of meat to be tossed into the foggy
skies, to catch it between your teeth
hold your head low but gaze fierce
as if you hold a solemn promise to all
who view you : you mean no harm
but are in fact scared of the force
a human can bring upon you. these
woods are your home, solace wrapped
in peace, only sound the cry of ravens
hovering in tree branches, sometimes
the howl which you lift your voice to.
the gray wolves around you are your
brethren, your pack. you pace and
linger near the bleached bones of
bigger prey. hip bone from an elk,
antlers of a skull. these are what
you have taken from the wild.
vital to the ecosystem, you are essential
and full of beauty. thick tail sweeping
behind you, lithe paws, and legs ready

to pounce on your prey or in play
with pack mates. your name means
wandering one, Nikai, and you wander
through the grounds with an eager
curiosity. an element of caution but
a fuel of desire to discover, to see.
you linger close to the gates but far
enough away that you can fade into
the backdrop, into the arms of the trees
if you need their embrace. I have traveled
far to see you and the vision of you renews
my strength. I will carry the image of you
within me
always.

"We travel, some of us forever, to seek
other states, other lives, other souls."

~ Anaïs Nin

LOVE YOURSELF WILD

~ a mantra

Love yourself—
radically and without inhibition.
Ask yourself to open your arms wide
Embrace yourself for all you are
All you have shown in every past reflection
Each journey that has led you here~
To this very moment
Where you can release all that holds you
Cages you and tries to make you tame
—Love yourself wild.
Love yourself when nobody else will.
When you begin to seek love elsewhere
First pull it from the endless wells within
Replenish yourself whole, as you always have been.
Remember all the aspects of you
Which make you feel that radiant love
Up from your belly, circling your heart
Wrap this warm energy around your soul
and know: you will soon be home.

When the universe reminds you
      how very small you are,

                        take heart, dear one
;   ;   ;   ;   your sentence continues on;

Indefinitely

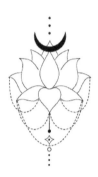

"Only you can crown yourself."
~ Guru Jagat

I

New Moon

I dance tonight

as many moths

without touching

down to earth.

CERISE LEAVES

give way beneath my feet as I navigate the forest. these woods are as much my home as any world of comforts. they shield me, protect me, welcome me with open arms. I travel alone—alone with my thoughts and the caress of wind against my scalp, weaving my hair into knots.

they say wolves travel here,
but I have never been afraid.

AMARANTHINE

There's a dream I have on repeat:
    I am flying, wings sprouting out
from my shoulders, feathers thick and soft,
lifting me into the air.

Weightless, the freedom of soaring higher
lifts up through my rib cage. But I reach too far,
brush the edges of the sun and my wings
      burst into flames.

I become a ball of raging fire, burning bright in the sky;
    I become the smoke and flame,
        a star imploding.

The angry lash of the sea beckons below—
    I know I will soon plunge
into its unforgiving arms...

        I startle awake as I hit its icy surface,
waters breaking around me like glass,
a greedy lover dragging me deeper;

wisps of smoke plume into the air,
black against an amaranthine sky.

CHRYSALIS

You are new. Reclaim all that was taken from you.

Shift; take on this form,
power; the control you have
sought for so long. you don't
recognize the girl left behind—
a ghost who helps define
the woman you become
but who is no longer
relevant.

Your dominance unfurls inside
like a flower, leaves budding,
petals opening, stem reaching   taller.

so many discoveries awaiting
beneath your skin,
begging to burst free.

NEW AGE

—haiku

Night wraps around me
 a cloak of sweat and fur, bone
 morphing into wolf

YOU FLOWER/ FEAST

I. *You flower*

chrysanthemum or valerian root vines leeching from open
wounds sticky like sap like honey smothering layers of skin

caught on my tongue in my teeth that honey sticky-sweet
sting of all the lies you spit open-mouthed weaving new infinities

grow roots deep bloom and burst and bask in the sun
it's what any good flower does (*promises broken like stitches*)

your seeds ride the wind thighs tight and cunt pulsing and
arched back and flight. you are a woman—say it again.

you are a woman.

II. *You feast*

on broken trysts discarded down drains slithering out
from spickets in spurts of rust-tainted water. you let him

touch you when it should be me. feast on his lust wheeze
deep around flower-filled lungs. breathe past suffocation

where all your memories sleep where lost lovers
wait for you to call their names once more in climax

on the places where you've made me bleed (*you woman,*
you woman) made me bleed this thing upon me howls

cutthroat melodies.

LUNATION RITUAL

On the new moon: find a space of
seclusion, embraced by seething wilderness.
        approach your ritual spot after dark
        guided by glowing light of an oil lamp—

Surround yourself with a magic circle drawn
in dirt.   Light a fire, heat iron vessel by its flame.

        Exactly at midnight, place in boiling water
        handfuls of:
                asafoetida, parsley, opium, hemlock
                poppy seed, saffron, solanum, henbane
                aloe, belladonna root, nightshade

Breathing deep the aroma, recite:
        spirits from the deep who never sleep, be kind
        to me / wolves, vampires, satyrs, ghosts! Send
        hither, the great gray shape that makes men shiver

Remove your shirt, massage skin with salve
        made from fat of a newly killed animal;
                aniseed, camphor, opium

        Pass a girdle made of wolf skin over
        steam thrice; tie around your waist.

Wait for the Unknown to manifest,
mysterious being. Dark blessing.

Touch lips to earthen ground
in reverent kisses:

Golden horned moon!

your change will soon begin...

LESSONS IN BEING HUMAN, FOREIGN

—found poem

things felt less foreign in the dark
everything smudged with human odor
dark perfume of tallow & incense
    our own scent/ foreign

dreaming of fatty & infirm elk
half-forgotten hunts/ eclipsed moons
we dreamed of rivers & meat

tongues curl around false new names
    (mouth shut, shoes on feet)/ we couldn't
return to the woods/ 'til we were civilized

long fingers of moonlight beckon
between languages/ a full
yellow moon smirked

pattern old hunger,   *(mouthshut*
    shoesonfeet mouthshut),   clawing its way
up my throat—wild-eyed, tongue
    lolling/ communal howl.

BECOMING THE WOLF

I become the wolf by birthright
born on the eve of Christmas when winter
nips at the doorsteps of villagers
waiting with breathless anticipation.

my path to transformation not by viral infection
swipe of claws or a bite deep in throat. I am born
into this curse & I am Other, slipping inside fur
like an ancient creature. bones pop

& clamor through skin. I grow larger—
more frightening, sharpen fangs beneath
glimmering moonlight like the beast I've always been;
these golden eyes hold secrets

to my shifting skins, living by
a noose of nocturnal nightmares
stalking through tall grass.
moon seasons demand I become

something more fierce than human flesh
I am the wolf, compelled to battle
all the hunters with sights trained on me.
awaken with bloodied fists curled

against my chest, fingers tufted with fur
twigs braided in my hair, mud-blackened feet.

my transformation, as usual, not fully complete
I always have a bit of wolf inside me

lingering deep, waiting to strike.
full amber moon marks this morphosis
more defined, lifts my snarling snout
in a chanting howl, a declaration to

all that exists within me, and all
that is waiting to exist.

BLOOD & CHOCOLATE

"I had the taste of blood and chocolate
in my mouth, the one as hateful as the other."
~ Hermann Hesse, Steppenwolf

the iron taste of blood in my mouth
melts down my hollow throat like chocolate.
after many moons spent racing through forests

I have mastered my craving for blood, heat
the taste of human like chocolate—a delicacy
divine. I feel relinquished after a kill

as if by being evil, I replace all good deeds.

the devil races through my hotblooded veins
beckoning me to join him, to maim
and murder the innocence that lingers

in my soul. I must have a baptism of blood
holy & ripe. freshly cultivated for my tongue
alone. this wolf inside me will not be sated

it yearns for flesh of men and women

it yearns for more than first requested
begs for a new beginning, crawling from

the womb cavity half-wolf half-woman

the way I was always meant to be born
& born again.

WOLF BONES

I struggle to leave the house alone.
as much as I am strong, I have become
a delicate, nocturnal creature.

I venture outside to soak my skin
in moonlight and howl, my voice rising
like smoke rings in the dark.

my fingers morph long and sharp
claws scraping at the marrow of cavernous cheeks.
I shudder and transform into more than human

all jagged edges, shedding curves like snakeskin
auburn leaves sprout from my head like loose
strands of hair flickering in the wind.

they crackle against ears morphed into a point
breasts budding beneath a layer of fur.
I have always wanted to embrace my own wilderness

take into the palm of my hands a ferocity
known only to the creatures bent into
bones and blood, away from civilized nature

reliant only on becoming whole.

I PRACTICE MY HOWL

in the shower, water streaming down
trigger-tipped skin. toss my head beneath drops
falling like bullets, unkempt hair tangled silver
arrowed brambles & rodent bones

bathing me in rubies, leather-skin crowning my
memory-etched bones. release, unclench a
travel-weary throat wrapped in barbed wire
and wince

past garbled words to find again my voice. to find
again my blood. to remember what was taken
from me, and all the pieces I must
puzzle back together.

MOON LIVING

2020

start tracking time by moon seasons
        (mon)soons   *mōna*
the full moon in March marks spring
the time i dig claws   deep in soil &
plant   seedlings of hope.   worms squirm
to the surface, wet earth   // scent lingers
heady, floral.   half-moon greets midday
sorrows,   a howl like rocks on my chest
      (the world is ending)   *apokalupsis*
yet i spend time in a garden
of glorious flowers.   (only exists in my mind)
the flowers are dry stalks snapping beneath
each step.   i can see them in a few months,
gentle heads   \\ swaying in a forlorn breeze
black eyes leering   between golden fingers
       a lone wolf woman wheezes
through the streets.   abandoned town &
the flowers still grow   weeds creep in to
suffocate, blind them.   *dens leonis*
roots sewn deep   // pluck their yellow
heads and still   they reappear. pale ghost
brother   *dæges ēage* (day's eye)
opens in the morning,   closes at night
gives birth to a   \\ new normal, new
generation. suckling dried lavender & sage
tied in a pouch, laid beneath   pillows

a glimmer of hope   glimmer of rebirth,
of spring reclaiming the land   warm breath
on my neck   a silent slumbering wind chime
      (together,   we survive.)
        the moon & i

LONE

forsaken, I belong to the darkness.

how many kills must I make, how much blood
stained across my fur, before this transformation

is complete? I become a lone wolf, abandoned
by my pack. no longer turn human by the light

of day. try to sniff me out, my home is the woods.
nestled in a homemade cave of branches & moss

this is where I have always belonged. isolated
at the mercy of my own being, I've lost the pack

who once surrounded me, guided me through
late-night hunts, away from civilization.

I lurk, at the edges of the city, dwellings full
of lethargic, sleeping humans—me & my

lycanthropic yearning for the Moon as my
guardian, my new religion & all that I have

left behind; that glowing orb in the sky is the
only mother I could ever ask for, the only one

I can expect to nurture me.

LADY OF THE LAKE

~ to the Great Blue Heron

she stands still in rapid riptides
sturdy on her feet as the current
ripples beneath her, flows around
her as one; feathered robe drips
turquoise into salient waters
the ebb & flow of her creation
an infinite bow to all that's divine
& all that remains pure within.

RED (AS A WEAPON)

I.

Cover yourself in red.

Red—multilayered and vast in both meaning and shade. Chartreuse or crimson, cerise or scarlet, maroon or vermillion, chili or rust or, even, lust. Red like the color of freshly drawn blood blooming from a wound. Red as a symbol of luck, good fortune. The life force flowing through veins—woman and wolf, both wild and tamed. Red for the blood that visits each month; red for your rage, hot and sharp, blinding; red for the color of your lips—lips that finally parted to speak truth after too many years of silence.

Smooth lipstick over their plump fullness,
admiring the vibrancy of color.

II.

Grow out your nails, paint them the deepest red you can find. Dye red streaks in your hair only you can see against the dark chestnut. Leave smears of yourself like blood trails wherever you go, the swipe of red nails and perfect red imprint of puckered lips.

Remnants—traces of yourself
like a trail of breadcrumbs
scattered through the woods so

you can find your way back,
though you only want
to move forward.

To forget memories left behind like those crumbs—the crumbs of
your trauma. Always following a few paces behind, marring any-
thing it touches.

III.

And for all your wolfen nature, you hold a love for fire dancing
deep inside your bones, the veiled excitement of watching things
burn. The release. The cleanse. Starting over, bright dancing beauty
of flames flickering deep in your eyes. The heat spreading from your
belly, up. Into your chest, deep hot ache.

You, too, can break out of this skin
and discover what lies beneath.

All while wearing red
like a cloak, like a shield
like a fierce weapon.

[BLOOD] LUST

I try not to think of the iron taste
painting the back of my throat
as anything other than
human desire.

II

Waxing

Even my human skin

can't hide the wolf within.

THE EARTH GIRL IS RE-BORN

baptized in water and mud of the Schuylkill
river water leaves my forehead corpse-cool

slick trails drip down my temple
    calming fevers left
      burning beneath flesh

I cover myself until skin
    becomes clay,

        step inside the kiln.

WAXING GIBBOUS

—for S.H.

warm soft noses and horse breath
steam the cold Danish air.
white bell drops hang swollen heads
toward deep earth and all is full—

where the ashes of a family lie,
the foundation of these rocky lives.

distant sound of a chainsaw nipping wood
of farmers working their fields and the
clop of horse feet through mud.

gentle cries of a mourning dove—I
want to ask, *what have you lost? does it*
          ache   the way I do?

sometimes I disappear just to see how long
before anyone misses me. I fade into
the ether and I really am the wolf,
this darkened creature of fur & teeth.

I linger outside homes where
smoke climbs toward clouds from stone,
where dusk and feathers fall from sky.

we all lose our footing sometimes. what matters
    is how we choose
    to rise.

WHEN I CHANGE MY NAME

I change it to something wolves can pronounce
hear it rising above treetops, hanging on branches
like skin, swirling carmine leaves in dizzy dances.
my name in their voices is magic, calling me home.

I am one with wilderness, nature exploding
from places hallowed in my heart. not just a woman
but a magnificent beast eager to grow, embrace
the power bursting forth from my split skin.

shed pelt to unleash the wolf, my sacred cry
joining with the rest, name thick on my tongue
as it eclipses the sky, growing bigger than my flesh
& bone body, the sound I emit defines the deepest

parts of me, rips from my throat and out
into the black night.

BLUE MOON

Learn to follow your instincts
even in the dark; eyes lit in body-heat
outlines—all the ways it means *to be alive.*

>   *I am changing*

in each moment, shifting skins
>   >   >   pasting on new masks
>   >   Oh, how we cling
>   to tattered pasts

>   >   *the   moon   is blue*

cheese, dripping from a heady sky
>   >   >   the taste of it is cranberry
>   >   My, how we sing
>   in symphony

>   >   *transform*

You always said I was a beast
>   you just never expected me
>   to become one.

CREPUSCULAR

I hunt at dusk and dawn
as the sun recedes, reaches
in bloom along the horizon

amber eyes absorb monochrome twilight
and each new day, my vision soaks in
red & yellow hues.

I travel many miles seeking food—
crepuscular hunter with many coats
my hair grows gray with time.

vespertine vixen

GROWTH

the rumble, like distant thunder, of trucks in the quarry
sifting through stones lined like ancient glaciers
rock formations chipped away one layer at a time,
  slate gray & amber & ochre.

here, the stream cuts a mouth through the forest-belly
tree roots hang loose like rotten teeth crumbling—
gaping maw, wide river-mouth, hungry salivating
   rush of spring water, dribbling, drooling.

clay on the bedrocks, the kind I used to cover my skin
as a child playing in Pennsylvanian riverbeds
seeking tadpoles and salamanders in the trees.

I grew in the desert with toes in the sand, cacti
racer snake dancer, tree climber. then I became
a woodland creature, hushed in the shade of
looming giants

   I tongued the world, earthen babe with silt
wrapped in my hair, turquoise marrow hardened
from a desert birth.

VARNISH

I paint my nails blood red, disguise the plasma
of my prey in their polish.   sharpen them to points
    pick from my teeth bits of skin & hair.
my heart thrums, palpitates like hummingbird wings.
breath tightens in my chest; I will never breathe again.
        / distort /
become the wolf lingering eternally beneath.
hunt those who make me quiver in dark memory.
one day I will become the thick sap painted
on woolen trees, something to replicate
what has come before, what has been lost
    to these woodlands.

as nightfall displaces daylight
my reign becomes stronger.   dark creature
of your nightmares,   I am here to reclaim
what has always been mine. these stones
hold the essence of my soul beneath
      your feet
burn your skin until you peel like bark from a tree
feel the pain you have caused unto me.
a strike of lightning will burn through you
scarring embers up your spine. I relish the moment
I'll sink claws deep into your flesh, tear
      the mask
from your face & strip you down so all can see
I am not the monster; it was you who couldn't be

believed. it was you who caused the ache
which will not leave my bones, dark thoughts
haunting my every day like vicious ghouls

I will eat the remnants of your soul,   digest
your dreams of fame. I will become greater
than you ever hoped of being. I will become
who I was always destined to be: great she-wolf
singing the song which vibrates the sky &
confessing your exploits.

GINGER SNAPS

after 'Ginger Snaps' (2000)

polaroids of dead girls & fake blood. staged suicides, sisterhood. we make a pact, B and I: *we'll die together.* on a full moon, new blood trickles down my thighs, its scent summoning the beast. becoming a woman bitten, four long scars carved across my shoulder sprout hair/ quickly healing lacerations. a tail buds from the end of my spine. *everything I look at tells silver bullet, gun to the head.* like a virus, I begin changing. white streaks my hair, bones split inside my arching back. my sister B pierces my navel with silver, sharp nail cauterizes the wound. I fuck a boy in the backseat, discover how hungry I am/ pass on the virus. growing fangs, hair thickens. blood oozes down my legs while shaving. whole body aches. after the first kill, I relish how good it feels—*warm blood on my hands*—like touching myself, I know every move I'm going to make. invincible, my skin ripples. all I want is to feast. less human. I've become the wolf, our pact broken. I'll die as B lives on, carrying deepest bond of our blood inside her.

LINGER

Existence is undefined;
I am at once part of the earth and sky,
lingering on the horizon in this fluid form.

moonlight licking dark pelt, his eyes find me.
I feel their heat kindle my bones like a
torrid touch promised, brush of fingers
along skin. *shiver / quiver / ignite.* like fireflies
greet an early spring moon, he gravitates,
dances over with swinging hips –
glimmering eyes deep-sea green up close.

a few shots thrown down thirsty throats
chill flowing towards heart. . . our eyes lock

my smile reveals the new hunger I feel clutching
at my ribs. he responds by leaning in; first kiss.

SISTERHOOD

the day my wolf sister   answered my howl
sparked my Soul back to life,   heart-fuse set
to burning   like a wild forest fire, unconfined.

when we howl to the wolves,   they lift their throats
to join, a short burst   of their powerful voices.
It is magic to my soul,   reawakening what
has been silent   but not forgotten.

*EIGI EINHAMIR**

I am not of one skin, taking on the form of many
while my gaze remains unchanged. shapeshifter in
variant forms, enchanting the sights of others
to look at me for what I am: the wolf, the wild
ever-changing beast who shifts
                              with eternal human eyes.

* *"not of one skin"; based off the Norwegian werewolf legends.*

ARMY OF WOMEN

I become a woman once I bleed,
once I ache deep in my womb
tremble throughout my bones.
my fight for retribution ended the same:
with blood trickling down my legs, unbidden
like scarlet lace tracing the origin of
my aching, absorbing my wounds into the
earthen grip of mud, feet rooted beneath
the soils. I become one with a forest of
ancient trees, arms outstretched as limbs
and hair no more than leaves and
winding serpents. melt down
from our waxen poses to become
something *other* than stiff sculptures
perfected by shaking hands. we stand
rigid, refuse to fall as we guard our
earth mother eternal and lead our
daughters, sons along the winding forest path
a trail of dead leaves & peeled bark-skins
shed from our naked bodies. we will be
gathered, stripped trees and pulp
circled around each other worshipping
each woven night, worshipping
the moon. whole in every phase.

MEDITATION MELODIES

Death is closing in at every corner
shivery tambourine of paper-thin leaves
dancing where they hang on long branches

harp of cattails in the wind, heads bobbing.
a bubbling background symphony, stream
carrying tunes between sturdy branches; *breathe.*

the lake shivers in crescendo, breaks like fingers
tracing gentle across its shimmering silver surface.

in the quiet, sheltered meditation of the forest
I find myself.

WOLF SONG

I train my voice to rise on the wind
embracing the sky in exultation.

My cries push through clouds that shroud
a cold moon glowing red-gold.

     Open your throat; let your voice join the wind,
     carried up to embrace the moon in each phase.

     Feel the rush of air against your nakedness as you run,
       the rough scratch of tree bark as you rush past.

* * *

To feel the fingers of wind thread my pelt
kiss my cheeks and the freckles
bursting across my chest. I am holy as
        the earth, divine as the sun and the sky,
        the stars and moon have drank me deep
as I have imbibed them, spooned silver
between supplicant lips; a solemn, solitary rite...

BLACK MOON LILITH

Eve, they say, came from the rib,
but I am of my own making.   a demon
of darkness, stealing babes for my own.
I am the night hag, a screech owl
shrieking through trees, flourishing
in this   empty   crypt. my feet are talons of
a hawk, clutching.   endlessly reaching,
seeking what remains obscured.
an inner darkness I attempt to shroud
but must embrace if I am to carry on,
this thirst for blood. pain. pleasure.
glory in the taking of what isn't
offered.   this is me: a creature reborn
of my own flesh & bone, umbilical cord
wrapped tight around my throat and
afterbirth flowing thick down my thighs.

VERSIPELLIS*

you will know I am coming by shrill shrieks
of birds fleeing in great swarms, wings flashing
through limbs in desperate attempts to escape.
they sense danger rolling in like a storm

before you could ever catch wind of me.
I am shapeless, a being of many forms
named in countless tongues. like a whirlwind
in its crescendo, I touch ground—light, fleeting.

destruction left in my wake, blood & sinew.
I wish to capture the form of you in my mouth
the foreign taste of you on the tip of my tongue
lingering in the back of my throat. forest birds

have already cried their warning of my passage
but it is your essence I've come to devour. it is
you whom I wish to capture in mind, body, spirit.
I will not be sated if I cannot soon claim you

for my next meal, suckle on meat making you
whole. learn all the creaks of your body, rivers
of blood and juice, the way you tremble beneath
me moments before I snap. delicate life force

draining slow from your body. a divine thing
to witness like holy communion.

this feast becomes my new devotion, courting all
that makes me most virulent.

* Latin, "werewolf"; adj. "shapeshifting, capable of transforming itself

or altering its appearance; sly, cunning, crafty"

SMOKE SIGNALS

we are here; where the first seed of me
was planted. a mere idea; an act of love.
my higher self invites me inside her tent,
"Sit crosslegged around the fire beside me
and travel deep" ~ smudges me in smoke
from a bundle of dried sage.

> we begin our soul affinity; speechless,
> focused solely on breath, until we hear
> echoing howls from the bowl we sit in;
> across the sides of great mountains eager
> to reach the constellations overhead.

> a red-tailed hawk swoops above,
> so I know my mother is watching
> over me as the wolves lift snouts in
> another spine-tingling serenade,
> reviving all that wishes most
> to be awakened.

THE RHYTHM OF THE OCEAN

HEALS WOUNDS

for Båring, Fyn, Denmark

my skin is rifted seaglass,
still sharp along the edges
but smooth in the center, shining
like hematite. grind me down
to red sand; witness the forms
this body can become.

WHEN THE FISH JUMP

I latch onto the shimmering sparkle of their tails,
each scale catching a kaleidoscope of rainbows
as the fresh river-water dances off its tongue
I can already taste the fresh meat in my mouth,
the way its bones squirm between my teeth
as I chomp down and feel the sustenance
of this river, thank it in gratitude & bow down
to this offering of life, a glorious feeling like flight
of the fish as it leapt into the air,
and the lucky wolf who caught it.

LA LOBA

she is a collector of bones, my wolf brothers & sisters
kept safe in her cave sanctuary, preserving what is lost.
sifting through the *montañas* and *arroyos* to assemble
a whole skeleton from many fragments, she carries
bundles of sticks on her back.
                                                her voice sings
over wolf bones, creates flesh & fur sewn on cartilage.
her song is magic, weaves life from oblivion, death.
whole wolf runs free over mountains, spectral creature
laughing woman streaking across the hills.
                                                known
in many tongues, woman of wolves & bone. she is
life where none exists, breathed into remnants
of the past like a dam breaking free to nourish dry land.
resilient like the desert, soaking moisture to hold
deep, conserve for decades in a drought & exist
against all odds, bend elements
to her great will
                                a survivor, witch—
bringing the dead back to life with melody
of her voice, tune hummed over stolen bones
bleached white by the sun. someday she will
collect me too, when my flesh has fallen away
& all that remains of me are shaken bones.
someday her spell will make me whole again.
she will bring me home, lay me down on a bed
of parched earth & cradle my broken pieces,
sing to me until I am reborn.

THUNDERSTRUCK

Let the rains fall down to cleanse me
~I let them wash this energy renewed~
Let them rejuvenate and nourish me
Full again. I shed my blood, absorb the
ache into my bones. Move my body
to the flow within, its inner tidal waves.

HOW A SHE-WOLF CHOOSES HER MATE

When we join bodies, we also join souls – a new kind
    of meeting, our heartbeats; our movements
all part of the rhythm of the earth, what we are meant
    to release, our desires and wants.

I want to capture the sound of you saying my name
    and hold it on my tongue, let it dissolve—
even now, I can nearly taste the heat of you

and when we climax together, the earth shatters,
    stars pop in our eyes
Our bodies shake and we clutch tight
    to our skins, anchored here.

after, we'll lie curled beneath
an endless twilight, stretching our arms
    to greet the dawn.

THE GATHERING

we gather in unity / hand-woven hemp
around our necks, decorating breasts.
tonight is one of revel / where we
cavil in moonlight & congregate.
take to the woodlands / the moon
as our mistress. some are guided to
dig mushrooms from earth / herbal
remedies. others stay behind to
guard our pups / tend the hearth with
brewed teas & henbane rituals; we
cover human muscle in handmade dyes,
mud-soaked leaves / wrap sodden limbs
around each other. before we became
our wild / we were weak, alone & sullen
now we are strong, bent down to four-limbed
rampages through shadowed city streets
testing our howls' echoes off barred windows
seeking out the quiet hush of forest paths &
the rush of midnight rivers / the taste of home
broken only by drums of our feet, souls
steadily alchemizing the twilight. We wake
in a pile of limbs / bodies swathed together;
each other's sweat, the crack of bones & teeth
licking our skins clean – no words are needed
our eyes speak / where tongues fall deaf among
fever dreams & heartaches offered to our alpha
exhausted only in this wild moonlit dance
ablaze with silver phosphorescence,
self-discovery, longing / love & destiny.

III

Full Moon

"*I am terrified by this dark thing*
That sleeps in me;
All day I feel its soft, feathery turnings,
     its malignity."

— *Sylvia Plath*

this is the belly of the beast &
I am eaten whole
to be digested / full of hopes
and dreams never realized
loss resides deep in my anatomy
a caterpillar in reverse / crawling
back to the earth / I will
regenerate through the soil,
roots up.

WOLF & I

So much heat; desire to break free and shed the judgment that still requests I care what other eyes will see, what other hearts may reject upon their own reflection... I watch my Shadow dance and match each movement upon the walls, a magic alchemy of air and fire. I am one with the wolf and my wilderness. I am the one I have been waiting for. This sweat and bone, back to the earth of me, back to the heart; the very thing that once begged creation — permission to be untethered, a wild beast biting at the chains within this body, I let her loose and set my Wild free to dance for me, to speak a language known only to spirits and the Soul that calls this Body home. Even the blood and tears of my ancestors, those who could not find a way to break free, the traumas passed from generations to be trapped here; I unburden decades of fear and pain, of "right or wrong" until I just Become—back to the very nature of all I am. The moon. The wolf. One.

WASP QUEEN

when the wasp queen stings,
her wisdom stays –   (venom)

splinters

I rub my back raw on the bark of a tree
its branches reaching like fingers to an endless sky.
these splinters have stuck inside me like scars
each time they prick me, it changes how I see—
my Moon, my mother. low she hangs in the night
how bright she lights up the darkness, hovering
like a compass, telling me to follow.
                                        so,
I'll rest myself on a bed of fur & bone
lick my wounds and try to tear the bark from
my pelt : it too has become part of me
it too is wild & fearless, grows on me
like a third skin.

INSOMNIA

wandering among moon-streaked windows
limbs swaddled in a cocoon of blankets
like a cavern; I become a woman walking in
moonlit woods – the wolf claiming my skin.

((howl again))

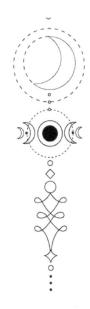

THE PLUM TREES

hung ripe with purple fruit
begging their juices be suckled
beneath the shade of the ancient
oak tree, rings inside telling an old
witness-story; we ate our delicate
lunch, plum juice running down chins
and basked in the danish air, the sun
that felt different, even the delicate grass
& the way gravity held me felt incredibly
sacred; a rite.

SINGING THROUGH MY WOLF BONES

"and as she fades before your eyes
I'll materialize."
~ Nuala Ní Dhomhnaill

under the gossamer balsamic moon   there exists
    my other Self –   gallivanting in the land
of Fairies;   an orphan kidnapped   *changeling*

you'll recognize me by the steady thrum   of music
    through my harp-bones   each vein a
different tone; softer than   before

            the memory of want
    eclipses me.   padding on forest-feet
each step an offering of *forgiveness,*   singing
    through my wolf bones.   my essence radiates

cobalt blue   as a railing ocean's   icy tide
        the moon its dominatrix, and mine.   this cyclical
shedding,   with each full rhapsody   renewed ecstasy

all bent to howls and   hot pokers through the throat;
    I begin to discover   the timbre
            of my own voice.

MY SERPENTINE

(SURRENDER)

Honor what calls you home.

Embody your power:
the fiery flames that ignite your soul,
the rains that come to cleanse;
the earth beneath your feet that grounds
& supports you, rocking you gently
through the solar system; the wind
threading through your hair, kissing your skin.

Embody each sacred element
and become one with all you are,
all that completes you & makes you full.

COMPLEXUS

I am wilderness. soot-smudged skin, mud-drenched limbs, cracking/ reveal what is underneath. *layers of masks.* shattered bits of broken hearts glued like a mosaic. my cracks filled with molten gold, an attempt to make me whole. worthier. I battle myself, claws and teeth.

I can be a wild thing full of fire and still emit light. heat. discover this beauty within, certainty. what else exists, racing through my veins.

BODY AS AN HOURGLASS

> *"The sun quits us; we are*
> *forsaken by light."*
> ~ Anne Carson

the body is an hourglass you can die inside.

[c. 1897, *hourglass* means *women's torsos* /
corseted ribs like bones of a cage, pressing the
body inside].

> a constant ringing in the ears,
> vibrations like pebbles.
> *time as grains of sand, moving*
> *through you.*

an hourglass you can die inside
might be a prison. . . but isn't time
a warden anyway? my body is a
Venus flytrap—one huge searching
mouth/ jagged steel teeth ingesting
all which tries to settle on my soft
pink tongue.

> i am an open wound
> flinching away from
> gentle offerings. a
> goddess's temple
> rejecting bounties laid before me.

the body is a refusal to behave.
the body is the felon and the
innocent. the free woman
and the enslaved.

what is life but a ramble through each phase.
i'm banging on the glass begging
to be let out, begging for the shatter.
i want my veins to bleed out their parched
sand. to open my palm and see jewels in my skin.
to hear the rush of rainwater, the promise
of a river.   to know i'll be washed away.

the body is a ship you seek harbor in,
breeching shore in strange lands. i have always steered
with desire at the helm. flying a red flag – *no mercy.*
fumbling my way through
dark memory like ghosts—
shadow-selves overlaid like
negatives /images in blurred frames.

ekleipsis—'a forsaking,
quitting, abandonment'.

we can shatter so easily, forsaken
by light. we can try to rebuild, but
there are always pieces missing, lost
fragments. *loss* fragments.   and i'm left feeling
along my body's acreage with bare-bone fingers, i'm
left picking up each shred   *i'm left.*   always the aftermath,
afterbirth. buried in the backyard to keepsafe the placenta.

the memory of what it meant to hold life inside,
the body as a vessel, body as a safe harbor,
body as a boundary crossed over and over
body as uncharted territories; body as infinite
beckoning, body as eclipse, body as body
body as soul.

MOUNTAINOUS

we thrive among trees that cling
to the side of great rock slabs

when we call, mountains answer
echo our exultant bellow

the elevation here screaming in our ears
pulses deepen. we obey earth's heartbeat

circle prey, tear them down with our
sharp teeth. the mountains

provide for us like a mother : shelter
warmth, food. peaked & full, rising

—I become the mountain.

PHOENIX FIRE

This internal fire seeds in my belly,
bleeds through my bones; feasts
with the relish of long-starved rage.
Moments of breaking apart/down,
this burning is a birth and creation –
the flames consume me 'til I am no longer
destroyed; I am whole, worthy
and I am delivered ~ a babe
of scarred flesh to be overlaid.

.:.

on red & golden wings of fire,
burning in a pile of ashes where I rise,
a wolf born beautiful in my fur pelt with flames
decorated down my sides, my hackles ablaze
I become a being of the wild forest, set free

.:.

racing into the woods, endless forests
of spit & teeth. I feel the hunger
of the earth beneath my paws, blooming
flowers become knives begging for
drops of blood.

.:.

I come out blazing. curls of smoke like
hair shrouding me. igniting the will
to continue living deep inside.

DIRE

I am the wolf dancer, danger
dripping from the tips of my teeth
my hips swing beneath thickened fur
tribal tattoo imprint wrapping
my thighs, undulating with

each movement. I've hunted down
my prey, blown the three pigs' houses
into bits and still, I hunger.

EVANESCENCE

like the *revontulet* fox fire in the northern sky
I dance, sparks rising from my paws as I run.

lightning without thunder, burning romantic
flames across the clouds. if I disappear into

darkest night, I will rise again, brilliant
beyond your wildest dreams. I am a creature

who belongs chasing constellations & stars
the evanescence of my being is a discovery.

you may think I disappear but I shift skins,
become something fiercer than you first

thought I could be. this fur envelopes me
in soft touch, excites me. hybrid soul

of legend & folk tales, existing beyond belief.
I sigh a final breath from convulsing lungs

my body spread across the night sky in cascading
stars, twinkling their infinite brilliance.

your children's children will look up & see
me chasing my tail, my grinning fangs

winking. they will follow my lead into

the hungry forest, become lost to you

forever, the way I have been.
the way I always will.

MEDUSA

submerged in sultry waters
breasts obscured by bubbles
floating candles, flickering light
of flame dancing across tiles
fondle moistness between thighs
hypnotized by jolts of pleasure
passion long hidden, now unleashed
like a sea monster rising up from the
bath waters, shimmering flesh of diamonds
rearing its regal head and capturing your
desires in one hot gulp, pointed teeth
steam breath on your neck, hardening nipples
clench your cunt and rise up, rise — exalt in
your solitary powers. your womanhood &
strength. a head of wild hair hissing tongues
of snakes, a single glance
will turn a man
to stone.

WOLF MOON

when the moon is round and full
unseasonal warm january night
feeding on this fever, down on all fours

don't be fooled—*this curse comes with a kiss*
we're howling forever. hair tangled with twigs

after a night spent running through woodlands
bare skin traced by thorns trapped in thick fur

my playmate, won't you lay hands on me

shroud me, hang a lunar anchor
offering your caress as a shawl of fragile lace

my mind's aflame
awake in human flesh coming home at 2a.m.

i know these wolf bones are embedded in me, thistle-
throated wail as i lay my soul in a bed of brambles

scrub my skin red, bearded moon lusts deep
blood on cream inside raw thighs

forest-scent deep beneath my claws
open my heart, let it bleed onto yours

BETTER TO DEVOUR YOU WITH

you tell me, *I've seen what your big eyes*
can do, I know how lethal they can be.
big brown eyes open wide, trapping you
like honey traps flies. and my big red lips
full & pouted waiting to be kissed, eager
to part and devour you deep; ravenous.

big razor-sharp teeth snap down on skin
undress muscles to gorge myself on bone.
my big thick ass, swaying hips :*thirst trap*:
you don't see the wolf tail hanging below
my peachy flesh like two orbiting planets
ready to be conquered. you're my catalyst,

the beginning of many devourings. I lick
my fingers clean of you, relish how your
scent lingers on my skin, bits of you stuck
beneath my long nails. I'll keep you there,
an afternoon delight, savoring every piece
of you left behind in crevices of my body.

WERIFESTERIA*

I gallop through forest
splashing in streams & creeks
water drops dance, beading on
spider webs strung between trees
sunlight filters through canopy
speckling my pelt, lithe form
weaving through trees, low rumble
of paws thump earth, dead leaves
crackle beneath each step, nose
in wind captures forest scents
chest blooming, heartbeat
the rhythm I leap to, boundless.
taste of air on my tongue
songs of birds in feathered ears
I am one with the forest, creature
undone, seeking to become
whole, leaves catch in fur
roll in mud, cover my skin in murky
lingerings. disguise the beast
in something other, innocent.
shift to soft skin, shivery—
submerged in crystal coppice
    I am Alive.

* *"to wander longingly through the forest in search of mystery."*

MY WOLF HEART

is a tethered muscle
like those broadening my shoulders
and rippling down my back, arching spine

into wild curves, becoming a four-legged
prowling beast of the night. my heart pumps
wolf blood through my veins. squeezes.

rhythm of my paws becomes a drumbeat
that I sing to the sky, triumphant, begging
nature to reply. it answers in echoes

telling me where to run, where to make
my home. this wild heart pines for you

SHEILA

~ after GLOW (2017)

I paint my canines yellow, slick back
short-shorn blonde; wig of wild black curls
a final touch in my transformation ritual.

know this with surety: my body is not for you;
what I do is not for you. I am she-wolf, rampant.
I answer to no one; fiercely loyal, deft and

agile in the ring. my body may be human,
but my spirit is a wolf racing through trees.

HE BECKONS YOU HOME

~ for my hubby

Peeling off long nails in the evening
to fresh baby-soft pink skin – a trail
of claws and acetone along the sink
bottle of silver polish clutched in
hand; and again, --- it begins.

in the morning, your husband says
he saved a claw from disappearing
down the drain. smiles as he kisses you,
your lips and then each fresh silver
human nail with   \ tethered lips /

each kiss, a
calling, beckoning you home...

CRACKED HEART OPEN LIKE A POMEGRANATE

Can you hear the howl
splitting out from my throat
cracked heart open like a pomegranate
its roots lick my belly, threaten
to climb loose ~slick as vines.
taste of cranberry thistle, milkweed
& poppy, sharp thorn of a bramble
pearled on my tongue, begging to be untangled
prick the soft skin of your finger laid in my
mouth; the pleasurable thrill
of delicate trust; lay your body
in the maw of danger.

DESERT WOLF

I strip skins to race naked over
desert sands heated by sun rays
my paws sink deep, conquests
beyond cacti, soldiers with thorns
in their sides, standing tall & holding
water, saguaro arms stiffened, proud.
I am a desert mongrel, wild creature
hunting by midnight murmurations, critters
burrowing down in dens. these parched lands
their home as they are mine: desert wolf
capturing the sun in my pelt, each
strand of hair vibrating with power.
when the desert cools white beneath the moon
I become a bolt of lightning streaking
along the split horizon, cool air threading
through my fur. within a shimmering mirage
I find my reflection.

MATING RITUAL

I teach him how to read the forest
and my body like topography
his fingers find each bump and birthmark
along the forest paths, my bare back
pushed against a tree, fur sprouting
along my spine as I howl into this throat
half woman cry half wolf—he pushes deep
between my legs, takes me against rough bark
weaving fingers in my hair, panting breath, clawed fingers
in his back and teeth in his neck (*awooo*). he licks
sweat dripping down my breasts, worships the salt
of my wounded body. he doesn't yet know
the wolf inside me, though he looks into her eyes
as we embrace, he sees the shadow of her pelt
when I turn and bare my ass in the air, he grips
her hips, pulls me in by his rough calloused hands.
he feels the savage inside me and claims it,
pounding me deep into earth's rhythms, a
glorious taking and tasting and twisting our limbs
tighter around each other, gasping lustful cries
filling the empty forest, mist-breath and magic
fogging the air around us as we confess our love
in great heaves, promise *forever* into each other's
cavernous mouths and grip tight to shaken lungs,
as we tremble, quiver, lie spent in our skins
on a chaotic nest of dead leaves.

WOLF BLEED

how many layers of blood can I shed
linings like skin peeling back and out
between my legs, a flushing of spirits
draining of souls, life-force flowing freely

twisted insides and sharp stabs.
i once heard: it's easier to put out cinders
than a raging flame – so I nurse the pain
before it begins; mark my calendar for
each moon-time when I declare myself
holy, again.

FULL MOON SHIBARI

loop silk rope around her thighs
hitch-knot and tie around the waist
harness clasped around her breasts
this is the way we tame the beast
caught in a jute net, unable to squirm free
this is her request – tighter, until the rope
leaves indents in smooth flesh. fur bristles
along her neck;   *unsheathe the wolf.*

LA PETITE MORT

the breath of me exhales
great puffs of steam like fog
igniting the air... as we climb
to the top of the mountain, steady
incline and heady elevation, we can see
the entire stretch of creek swaying through
endless trees that reach to grasp the universe.

before I could die, you brought me back to life
resuscitated my heart with oxygen from your blood
and gave me the gift of hope, to carry on.

now I feel ready to experience many little deaths
in the safe cradle of your arms, the rhythm of your
heart rocking me gently like a boat upon
the waters of eternity.

LUTEAL PHASE

I mark growth by the patch of hair,
curled tight between my thighs & my
moon cycle, the way time seems to ache
like a seed taking root in my abdomen, wrapping
tight around my ribs the way fog winds through trees
forsythia blooms in vibrant fury, golden fireworks
bursting beneath the trees. spring arrives full roar
a rising in me like the tides as my moontime comes
upon me, sweeps me down & under. I grow quiet,
more tuned to the inner workings, inner power of
creation roiling like the northern lights swirling fire
in the Norwegian sky. I writhe & dance and move,
become more intuitive – liberated – when I let myself
embrace that freedom, shed my fear of judgment
back to the wild soul callings & self.

IV

⁓

Waning

the *aurora borealis* may not flow your way
but let their brilliant light illuminate for you a path
to find a way home to that radiant ocean of
blues and grays and black, the spray of it upon
your face and skin, the salt licking across your face
a promise in the wind that you'll feel all the love
I possess within my bones upon you, someday. I will it
and so it may be true.

BONE-WHITE BLEACHED BIRCH BRANCHES

rise like driftwood biting from sea foam,
like looming gravestones marking the dead.

in the gloaming, fading light hits tree bark
kaleidoscope sheen of feathered patterns
cascade onto my pelt and I am home

among the trees swaying in gentle breeze
carrying cries of ravens soaring on wings of air
promising shelter & warmth as they stretch

higher than I will ever grow into raging sky
I am a creature made from bleached birch
I am the driftwood in your teeth, the headstone

with your epitaph: *killed by wolves*
and the howl, and the crunch,
and the cry, and the night.

CRESCENT

I feel tonight's crescent blossoming
    in the crevices of my bones, song of
        my marrow burning loud & cold like

steel lighting a silent night on fire.
    my heart dredged beneath dark tides
        brimming deeper with its ache. I

hide in a shroud of smothered desire.
    no longer wishing to surface over clouded
        waters, I drown these shifting skins

until my reflection gazing back ripples
    into a thousand shards of who I am.
        the way Hecate smuggles the heavens

with each night I will steal from you
    the lifeblood in your veins. I worship
        every part of myself: broken & beaten

pieces, the wholeness within.
    move onward at reckless pace
        seeking infinite ignition of my soul.

moon waxes above & I wane, racing
    along forest paths, howl burning hot
        in my throat, eyes wild with wanting.

GRIEF

is a strange animal.
it wakes you at all hours
with vacant howls, dreams
that wisp away like cobwebs,
sticking always in the corners.

.:.

if you don't answer,
    it will continue its howl.
waking you with shivers
        waking you in fits
the ghostly eyes of lost loved ones
        hanging in cavernous sheets

your memory & aura captured,
painted in windows like stained glass
indigo, rouge, rust, and turmeric

OUR LOVE

is wild, rash, raw—full of passion like wild berries
popping under teeth, juice flowing over tongues
the way we inhale each kiss, the way we taste
each other, hold deep your breath in exhale, gasps
released in moans, in ecstasy. our love is
not always requited, full of lies, full of holes.

it is not whole.

it is rough, ragged, bone-dry. begging for sustenance
a thief running through the night, heart tucked
like an egg carried in a fox's mouth—delicate,
trembling heartbeat beneath shell. one slip of teeth
and life will ooze over thick-tongued promises.
where there is no love to offer, you continue to give.

WHEN I AM THE HUNTED

they hunt me by the yellow light of moon
I am a monster plaguing their village
consuming hearts of innocent residents
& feeding off the foolish bravura of men

I am what legend makes me—a primal
pariah, misunderstood. I refuse mercy
take my victims full by their thick throats
now held delicate between teeth. one snap of

my jaws and their lifeblood flows inwards,
wolfsbane beckons further, new identities.
only silver bullets embedded in my heart
could stop me forever, otherwise I remain

in many lifetimes. I will rise, as if incarnate
again, so long as the birth is worth the pain.

BY THE ROOTS

when we cut down a tree /start closest to the roots
I pull out strands of hair /eyebrows and lashes
their ends white like the tails of fleeing deer
or rabbits down a hole

listen for the crash /vibrating through
earth –each action has an effect /rippling

all those twisted roots exposed /pieces of myself
come undone /pearlescence from the moon
reflects on opal skin /stars are strings of pearls
hanging from the delicate neck of night

tree rings mark age like wrinkles edging eyes
how long I have tried to heal /how long
tall forest guardians have soaked the sun

these tears pour down like rain /ready
to nourish something greater than me

I GROW MY WOLF TAIL

thick & bushy
bursting from the end of my spine. balancing act
brings me back to ancestral times. Wagging my hips
feeling the tug of earth on my behind, the promise
of muscles above my thighs.

so let me take that gentle paw and swipe the earth
let me create a path through winding woods for you
to journey beside me. I've been a lone wolf so long
I no longer recognize what it is to have another
match my thick strides, two sets of paw prints in dirt.

I try to catch the moon on my tongue
             like a drop of warm milk
weaving through trees with eyes fixed.

I travel to a planet with many moons
             hovering above the horizon.

these moons share the sky with a burning sun.

my pelt is ablaze with heat as I leap through
craters. one day, I will be a wolf in Neptune's orbit.
I will be the wolf dancing on Saturn's rings.

*take me to your secret grotto of the woods where
hope grows thick on trees and the water sings
near-forgotten melodies.*

WHAT THE FOREST TEACHES US

there is beauty in the hushed moments
when wind rustles tree branches &
small creatures scurry in undergrowth—
not a single moment is complete silence

when wind rustles tree branches &
life flourishes everywhere, each hole
(*not a single moment is complete silence*)
and crevice of the forest is full, in bloom.

life flourishes everywhere, each hole
there is peace in the sun dappling
and crevice of the forest is full, in bloom.
down from the overhead canopy,

there is peace in the sun dappling
a fresh breath in each padded step.
down from the overhead canopy,
like trees we rely on those who stand strong

a fresh breath in each padded step.
whose roots reach to tangle with ours
like trees we rely on those who stand strong
and we share our light, this deep connection

whose roots reach to tangle with ours
and sunshine dances across skin & fur
and we share our light, this deep connection

gives us reasons to keep growing

and sunshine dances across skin & fur
until we finally find: *home*
gives us reasons to keep growing
among our kin, breathren.

until we finally find home
small creatures scurry in undergrowth—
among our kin, breathren;
there is beauty in the hushed moments.

WOLF OF WALL STREET

a silver tongue seduces prey into selling slices of their souls.
well-kept in pressed suits and ties—you'd never see the fangs
just by looking but they lurk beneath that predatory smile,
throbbing vein at the clavicle/ lampshade lids cast over a
candlelit gaze. room in a fancy hotel for a single night, silk sheets
slide beneath limbs tossed free/ a different kind of forest romp
through stockbrokers & money—sweet bouquet of
temptation/ sweetest drug the wolf has ever known/ feasting
on eternity but coming up empty each spin/ nose dusted
in stardust. sometimes addiction is a mate that won't quit you
a creature more cunning than lions or tigers or bears
once your scent is caught it's learned for a lifetime
and all you can do is try to run/ cheat Death & the law
a haze of skins/ bodies bared for base pleasure/ all this
taking will never fill you/ wall street already ate you alive
spat you out like a sour dream/ all that's left are clouded
declarations of *what could have been*: sweet-sugared tongue
devil eyes/ knots at the throat/ striptease of sacred loss

just out of reach.

EXSANGUINATE

~ after 'Unleashed' (2004)

the faster you heal, the closer it gets, B.
I bloodlet and track how fast the tissue heals
shooting wolfsbane in my bloodstream
like an addict, purple poison. soon it will come
for me, no matter where I hide. it finds me
in the sanitarium, it finds me in the woods.
I must keep shooting wolfsbane in my veins
or else I will turn into the beastly Other
which claimed my sister—she haunts me still;
appears to remind me just how bad it's going
to get. my notebook fills with marks, how fast
my self-inflicted wounds begin mending,
how much humanity remains before
it will be too late, like Ginger:
I must embrace the wolf inside me
        unleash the beast
        and set it free.

A HUNTRESS'S TALE

~ for Diana, and all who hunt with purpose

I. *I hunt*

therefore i am/ long lone hours huddled in underbrush
lurking/ sniffing out weakened prey. i take for sustenance

use each part of the animal i catch/ chew on bones/ mount
antlers like trophies. thrill of the hunt awakens deep muscle

early winter rush of breath, clouds hover over a silent earth
path i travel gives way beneath paws/ crackling leaves.

II. *Surrender*

the elk before it leaps, white flag waving in the air.
startled scarlet pheasants like firecrackers erupting sky

aim & steady/ hold/ *release*—I go off like a trigger
kill falling across my feet/ fresh meat bounty.

TO THE DOE, ROTTING

your ribs are bare on your chest cavity
where I imagine your heart was homed
is that what the vultures consumed first?

the vital organ that once pumped blood
through your leaping body, long legs kick
up in joy, in life. you must not have seen

that death machine hurtling toward you
before it was too late, and you became
a once-vibrant thing reduced to fur and

dead eyes on the side of country roads;
scraps to be eaten, a meal for the birds
circling above. all I can think as I pass

is how this is the way I have been left,
a dead thing to be devoured or scraped
up from the pavement. glass eyes gaze

into the distance but I will never dance
through the forest again or nibble on
ripe stalks of corn. maybe this was a

kinder way to go rather than staring
down the barrel of a rifle & knowing:

t h i s   i s   t h e   e n d.

SKINWALKER

I am the offspring of sorcery, great astral body
a tickle in your chest, fluid in your lungs
death rattle clawing from your throat
I feast in darkest night wrapped,
a cloak of fur. take on my second skin
bury my humanity by the bubbling brook

where I lost my purity one moonlit evening
rolling naked in the mud, in your arms.
I didn't know then how the mud would
become my skin too, lodged beneath long nails
brambles snagged in the fur at my neck
so now I snap, bite & maim lone travelers

under the watchful eye of great oaks. when
you penetrated my soul, you didn't know
I would become this great creature like those
who haunt the *hogans*, fluid spirit who can
wrap around you & constrict, claim you
with the moon as solo witness to your plight

I dig deep into graves of the dead, exhume bodies to
smuggle their jewels & bony fingers, concoct
lethal potions that will cause you to waste away.
I come upon you slowly, patient, easing into
poisonous view, slow whisper of death draining
all the strength from your tired bones.

skinwalker, I masquerade in this human shell
a forest blooming from my veins like roots.

WOLFPACK

we run as a pack, fur brushing against each other
feverish with the moon at our backs, pushing us
forward together. we are waves of the ocean
crashing against the sand, tides driven by the tug
of the moon—our Goddess in arms, glorified & elegant.
we answer to each other's keening, swim through our
collective scent. stronger as one, our thoughts
roam as a single thread, whispering moonlit secrets
between ourselves without a word spoken.
some of us young, full of energy & clumsy
in our fur, paws padding across forest floor
earthen smells fill our noses turned to the sky
our voices rise, circle our mountainous home
we hunt as one entity, fur rippling over muscle
our human instincts disappear as we crave meat
gristle & bone. teeth snap, taste air as we trace
scent trails of rabbits, deer, woodland creatures.
only some of us have the forbidden flavor of human
lodged in our jugular, a scent we never forget,
pine and woodsmoke taste that lingers long after.
wolves rarely survive on their own, the pack becomes
everything. we yip, roll, play, growl, live as one.

COLD AS STEEL

"Bright is the moon high in starlight"
~ Metallica, 'Of Wolf and Man'

the night I go to him, the air holds a chill
reaching deep beneath my fur, cold as steel
the moon shines high above, full-bellied.

> *Out from the new day's mist*
> *I have come*

I want him to see me for who I am, the wolf
not the woman. crouch outside his house
hidden among the pines, light flickering

inside his workshop. even in the dead of night
he whittles away at his wolfen figures.
I want him to carve me, watch his hands

> *shift // pulsing with*
> *the earth*

mold my body out of wood, imagine his fingers
running along my curves, jolts of electricity.
how he smooths me out, scrapes deep into

the marrow of me, harnesses my wild beauty.
I creep closer to the shed, ears pricked for

a sense of movement, on alert.

(shape shift)
nose to the wind

there is something, a smell in the air
a low rack of a shotgun being pumped
he stands in the door of his woodshed

points the gun between my eyes
dead-shot, aims his weapon with steady
hands, those fingers I've admired.

call of the wild
fear in your eyes

he moves to grip the trigger
moonlight bathing us, first sight.
I lunge, tackle him to the ground

rush of breath tickles the hair on my
neck as we fall, roll hard together;
he begs & whines. I make him silent.

back to the meaning
of wolf & man

LURID

~ found poem

turning the night lurid—carnival light.
sparks took place of stars
a silhouette fronting hell
    consumed in fire.

toward the woods
night-clothes smeared with soot
faces white with terror.

a woman wailed
and wailed,
    "They burned us out."

the roof collapsed
in a peacock tail of sparks
and flame.

    too late.

MORRÍGAN*

I am an ancient shape shifting goddess, longing
to gorge on his loaded heart. journey many miles
to savor him, through deserts & canals, rush of
water pours across many skins, thin husks;
dry heat warms my pelt, revenant moon.

> *they say I bring disease & famine, leave bite*
> *marks deep in prey, but I am so much*   *greater.*

my wounds weep, beg to be licked by his
thick tongue. salivate for me a healing balm
& expel the filth from this celestial being.

an ancient thing, beast untamed
I will never be the same as I once was—
forever changed. hunt me like a witch-wolf   (*mac tíre*)
condemn me to the stake.

I continue to shift,
unable to remain only human.

* *From Irish mythology; literal translation "phantom queen"; a triple goddess,*
said to transform into a red-furred wolf before battle.

WAYFARER

I have seen inside of you
viscera splayed across the forest floor
lungs & heart & veins
caressing pieces of you in my claws
careful not to pull you apart
all I ever wanted was to keep you
whole. I never wanted
to see you broken before me
yet this is how you appear
how you've always been
unwilling to give any part of yourself
over to my love. instead I take.
I kill. I never wanted to
hurt you. if I could stitch you back
together, I would. though I fear
I will never again form nimble fingers.
& still, the sanguine taste in my throat
fills me with a lust I have only now
discovered, a craving that can never be
satisfied. I'll continue answering
to it, a monster fully formed of desire.

RAPTURE OF WOLVES

~ an acrostic

we are constellations, cosmic dust
once weaving through the night sky
leaping within space & time. we are more than
fathomed, more than we have ever known

revolving on Saturn's rings, Alpha moon ascending
a rapture of wolves chasing our tails around
peeling bark of stars, the moon our lighthouse
tracing beams between tall guardian waves
under light of glorious apocalypse, glowing
radiant among all darkness of our inner cosmos
existing beyond any understanding.

TENEBROUS

I want to breathe again those silver moments
like starfish found clinging to a sea-swept rock
hanging on for dear life, or just soaking up sunshine
and I want to cling too, to moments where I suck air
deep into my lungs and feel my whole body l i f t
into the sky, my feet come off the ground and i am
a spirit, sepulcher set free from rooted stone
one day i will look at my reflection and see, i
have been whole the entire time, waiting for
my eyes to clear.

INDELIBLE

they found elk bones in the woods
scarred indents of my teeth, savage.

what they will never know is how I
scrape meat & marrow, slash tendons

to gorge fully on flesh, ravenous & eager
jaws darkened like claret from my prey

fur matted, woven with twigs & leaves—
forest debris now part of me. I leave behind

bare skeletons scattered along forest paths
crows circle overhead seeking scraps

ears perked for the sound of snapping brush
hunters lurking between trees hoping to

snag the wolf, become a hero of the village
those mountain predators, rolling muscles

sharp snapping teeth & brutal fangs
I am unbound, unleashed; indelible.

RESILIENCE

We rise like the tides persistent against shore,
ever-changing peaks foam in silent salute
to humanity's resilience.

Look back at all we have survived, all that
carries us forward now, enduring; holding
our hearts steady, cementing love
as a community.

We are survivors, waging unseen wars,
discovering over and over the brilliance
of our spirt – unwilling,
yet again, to break.

V

Half Moon

*"And the day came when the risk to remain tight in a bud
was more painful than the risk it took to blossom."*
~ *Anaïs Nin*

I am half-transformed:
a woman of flesh &
a wolf of midnight fur

try to catch me or tame
the wolf within, I won't be
claimed or caged

I am mine,
and mine alone.

HUNGER SWELL

i. Crimson

cloak, I track the girl with her hood pulled low
scent of innocence & wonderment. she traipses
through without notice or concern. I fight a twinge of

hunger & bile in my throat. she does not know
wolves lurk here. she doesn't know what she will
discover walking this path, how close she comes to

knocking on Death's door. her clumsy steps
crash through fallen leaves coating the forest
floor, she does nothing to remain quiet. nothing

to hide her passage, as if she owns the right
to be among the woodlands, claiming stake
on my land. I wish to teach her a lesson—how

savage, how unforgiving I can be. I let her
pass by, crouched low in the undergrowth.
watching her, the way her hips swing beneath

long woolen cloak, how her dark hair cascades
over one shoulder beneath the hood, her red lips
pursed like a rosebud, petals ready to gently open

ii. I can no longer resist

barrel out from brush to tumble her over;
she screams in surprise. I trap her cries in my throat,

mauling & biting; rip her to pieces with unforgiving
claws, consume her whole until we are joined as one, *no*

separation between woman & wolf, skin & fur molded

her blood flows from pale perfection, stains me
so I soak in her beauty, she becomes my pain

personified, the hollow echo of an empty heart
as I destroy every bit of her, torn to shreds

until she is no longer moving, pale limbs stiff
all the color drained from her face; lifeless eyes.

iii. All the good girls go to hell

& the sunlight is woven in my pelt
like delicate strands of gold.

I leave her on the forest floor, tug her thick body
between my teeth, bury her beneath a bed of leaves

& cover her face with a shroud. *I am layers of masks*
I take her smooth skin as my own, shift from wolf

& stand, a naked woman covered in warm blood
slide the crimson cloak from her shoulders & swing it

to embrace my own, stand on shaking legs, walk
down the path, *woman or wolf?* I no longer know.

I no longer recognize myself or the beast
I have become. my reflection dead behind me

like Vesta, my eternal fire turns faith to
scarlet ashes clotting beneath clawed nails.

reawakened, I forge on through this thicket
dodging thorns starved for savoring skin.

STORMCHASER

Rain soaks my pelt, quivering skins
shake & shudder deep, caught between
shifting beast-woman woman-beast
snarled fangs & sweet smiles morph

when did I become so blood-thirsty?

Yearning to sink my claws through skin
deadly bite at the neck, ripped throats
always screaming for mercy I won't give
the only Man I thought could love me

tried to kill me. couldn't see beauty
beneath wolf skin. my golden eyes
hang like a new moon, luminescent.
passion often wasted, unwanted

why did I think he could see me?

my lone bark echoes off trees & mountains
my destiny is to remain a l o n e.
crying for what I have lost, Moon my
spectator, darkest night my blanket.

when storms rock the earth, know
thunder is the rumble of my feet
trampling miles to hunt you.
lightning is the flash of my soul,

seeking chaos, wind an aching moan
bursting free from my raw throat.

MAROON

when I die, bundle my bones
burn this human husk to ensure

the wolf part of me is dead, too.
take my ashes and bury them

in the woods, where I was happiest
sprinkle them along the creek

so I become one with the bubbling
waters where I used to drink, long tongue

lolling from my mouth, where I bathed
in half-wolf form, crystals of water

clutching at this changing skin.
I will exist always in the wind

on a full moon where my howl rises
to fill the stillness within you. cry of

the wolf, the call of wild that screams
inside all of us. my spirit will always

race between the trees like one endless
looping thread, a redness that returns

in   fallen   leaves.

NO WONDER POETS FALL IN LOVE
WITH THE MOON

I.

I am just as blemished, my skin full of craters
pocked by winds of time, scars of my travels
lodged into delicate flesh. poke holes in me
like intricate lace. I still remain whole, even
if half of me glows gently in the midnight sky

II.

the moon becomes shrouded too
by earthen ashes, clouds of sorrow
wrap around its slick waxen body;

I want to hover over the world
with as much strength as the moon, a
goddess in my own right, mystical

and full of light.

WRECKAGE

"I came to explore the wreck."
~ Adrienne Rich

I stand there shivering half-in my fur, half-out
wishing I could be anywhere other than
on the side of the highway with cars rushing past
every single driver straining their necks to
look at me. bloodthirst reflects in red taillights
flashing—*blink, blink, blink*

no matter how far I travel it will be at my back
hovering like a demon latched atop my shoulder.
naked skin or furred, I am the same: brilliant
bright beast burning and flaring in the winter light.
red coat wrapped around me like a fourth skin
my armor, my shield. wolf instincts howling out
into darkness, begging to be heard, a bidding
and a warning.
a call to say: *I'm on my way.*

I don't know where I'm going, but I'm traveling
discovering my skin, trying on the fit of new souls
and always on the move, just out of reach of
the beast's claws, who trails behind me, lurking
and lingering—sometimes right on my tail
and others just a shadow in the trees, just a

shadow.

I'm bathed in a world of strange lights
floating in moments of liminality. I don't cry
because I'm dreaming of racing through woods;
freedom, the cold air on the nape of my neck.
I don't pull my fur on because I know
they'll see the ferocity inside me, they'll
        throw blame.

the only human who sniffs me out
is the man who drives my battered car to the lot
the one driving the tow truck who calls me sweet
his voice a soothing wind blowing over raised fur.
he brings me inside the warm cab of his high-bed truck
and only then do I pull on the cloak of my fur
        safety, warmth.

I bare my fangs at him so he knows
who I am, and he sees it—   the devil in me.

MY BODY

feels like a coiled serpent, prepared to strike - power circling in my muscles; a sturdy oak rising among a forest, swaying in a gentle breeze and whispering my secrets to the wind; a delicate unraveling rope as I puddle to the floor, release the tension of my limbs and break my bonds which limit movement. . . my body feels like a river, satin water flowing as I allow myself to float downstream; a solid rock grounded into the Earth; a mountain rising above desert lands. like an ocean, waves of emotions dragging me deep, holding me steadfast until I burst free from the surface sputtering love notes as music. like a map, each scar and mole create terrain to trace, memorize and learn, continually leading me home.

tastes like Palo Santo smoke and candles streaming through the air to lie trapped on my skin: warm vanilla and cinnamon. tastes of salt from tears and sweat; the deep iron of blood being shed in a new death which evokes rebirth to rise. The taste of dreams if they had a flavor, and desires ready to lift off into the ether.

smells like the tang of spice and pine; fresh air caught in strands of my hair from a wintery walk in the woods. The aftermath of a fire lit from within; dragon's breath and lavender oils rubbed into skin.

looks like a rose in full-bloom, so very alive with a blush across my cheeks, smooth skin marked by blemishes and scars, imitating beyond the ordinary - freckles that appear more often in summertime, hibernate in winter. reflects internal beauty, a shining emblem of hope and all the embers we have walked through; weight appearing again at my waist and thighs. looks like an offering to some but to me, it is a haven, refuge in every storm.

sounds like a drumbeat, each rhythm of my heart vibrating through veins. The breath flowing through throat and lungs a whistle, a rushing stream over rocks worn smooth. creaks as I flick each wrist, protests with a whine as I lift it into shape - asanas and mudras to remind me I am sacred as I fold, twist and dance. The steady sound of my feet as they break bread with the earth, the rush of my fingers across the keyboard, a calm lullaby of truth and creation. My body is music, a serenade.

INNER BEAST

I am born half-beast
stretching out my skin, bones
constantly shifting, cracking
beneath the weight of
growth.

I will continue transforming
into any shape possible, never
an end to how large I become
encompassing all space
in your heart.

my trembling desire always
reaches vast; I am changing,
a fluid being without limits
discovering new yearnings
every day

making amends with this
internal beast, baring fangs
emitting a low growl
to remind me, I am never
alone.

MORE WOLF THAN WOMAN

even in dreams, my feet race through woodlands
breaking twigs beneath each step; trees fly past
as I heave breath, deep. legs burn with heat,
my heart pumping like a shotgun begging for relief.

even in dreams I gasp, claw, pounce & roll.
I wonder if I am now more wolf than woman.

I can no longer resist my wild nature; bare teeth
on the sidewalks, hackles rising at the back
of my neck. becoming something vicious.

I've lost myself to a Wolfen nature
dominated by the call of the Moon, its willpower.

hunt, prey on victims, small and trembling
in their soft skins. my fur bristles when I come alive at 3am,
my own beast trapped in a world of wickedness.

visitor of the night, captive to the evil thrill
of my heart thrumming to its body's vibrations

of my soul, the hunger of a wolf, the taste for blood,
a dark desire inside myself I can no longer deny.

ROAR OF TRUTH

splits from my throat, its roots finding home in my belly. I find my voice again and again, after losing what I thought was mine; everything that belonged to me can never be taken away - my voice among the most dear. I always knew I could howl as high and long as any wolf, roar as fierce as any lion, and sing as delicate as a bird - true notes of "I love you", until I found the One to say it to (*'jeg elsker dig'*). Embers from the pit of me rush up and out my throat - I am both fierce and soft as I find my tongue, honest and bold. Even when my voice shakes like the earth trembles, I find my way back home to all I am within, light a steady fire in my gullet and breathe out flames into frosted air.

WOLF WHO EATS THE UNIVERSE

my silver coat blends   with snow
in ice and wind, my howl dances
joining   sky like lightning, flashes
its ignition, what keeps me burning
despite frozen grounds around
my wolf pelt,   wise old eyes and
extra layers of fur. I am one   with
the earth beneath and when I lift
my snout into the air to join the call
of my brothers & sisters, I open a jaw
ready to snap hold of a whole world
take it   between my teeth and crush
until it filters down my endless throat
fills me and my desires so I could never
want for anything again. when I consume
the universe   it is so I can discover
what love really tastes like and how I
can become   my own exquisite gravity.

KICK A HOLE IN THE SKY

~ found poem

could they see the forest
in her eyes, the shadow
of her pelt?

an outsider, unwanted

*I can run with the night
and catch the dawn.
          I can kick a hole in the sky.*

the forest a wild thing

red slashed into the dark—
eyes, blood.

          loup-garou

through pooled moonlight
by ritual, sacrifice,
sacrament.

abandon knives of flint

use teeth/ beast within
subject to the Moon

more than human.

FOLLOW YOUR FLAME

I came from the wastelands
of trauma and pain, of numbing
to all reality, denying myself existence
only to walk out of the embers, untouched
by the heat – born from the ethers of smoke
a candle infinitely burns, beckons you closer
the flicker of dancing flames the most
     sacred
     seduction
the pillar of the mind bending to the winds
unseen yet known; unheard yet felt, always asking:
come nearer, go deeper. listen to the forces calling
you home, listen to the ancient desires
and requests of all who walked before you;
a daughter, a sister, a beloved ... wound into one
essence, one being, one soul.
I am just *me* now, trekking ahead,
no longer afraid of what leads me,
no longer fearing the warm embrace
of all it means to live. all it means to give birth
to our ideas, the greater laws of the universe.
each journey guides us deeper, renewed... the
momentum captures our spirit and asks us to return
release, rejoice. for always in the silence exists
another lesson, a whisper of solace and
newfound wisdom... carried ahead into any storm;
I am ready to be born over,
ready to be bare.

MY FUR BEGINS TO SHED

in patches
great tufts pulling out between my claws
covering the forest floor
I have turned into a soft thing, human skin
curled among scattered leaves and moss

when weakness grips again my skins
and I am shrouded in broken limbs
the storms hit hard, no quarter
raking me to severed pieces while I beg
for mercy, for relief

while I beg the wolf to come
save me from the soft-skin days
when I can no longer race through woods
or feel the caress of wind in my pelt
where I can no longer see beauty

and all the flowers in the meadow shrivel
all the creatures who were once playmates
have grown weary and cold
the earth is dead beneath my paws
eternal mother no more

there's still life in you, a question mark
asking you to turn your face to the sun

METAMORPHOSE

a renascence of love
as droplets fall upon flesh
dancing beneath thunder, a
lightning flares internal; kindled
by the drops like rain-kisses
invoking my soul to venture out
from her cavern, hollow throat
and open heart to all the world
offers - revived, reincarnated
beneath warm waters, splash of
cold to transform each nerve
into feeling, breathing, exalting
anew. a persistent, tenacious
grip on what it means to cleanse
and restore belief. absolve me
of past sins, transgressions of
self-abandonment; one certainty
I've discovered without doubt
is who I am, who I want to be
and all I can become.

EQUINOX

when day & night become balanced
the sun's light stretches to meet
its yin of the moon arching to peak

the wolves howl a serene song
activated by the bulbous moon (*shine*)
equinoxium ~ we are all full of duality

just as the equinox reminds us. my heart
is deep purple, veiny as worms who relish
in an afternoon rain. a sheath of protection

there's a man walking with chains looped
around shoulders: but I am not ready to be
re-caged. Offer me a sanctuary

to rest my weary soul. a gentle compassion
glinting in the fallout of the roar.

RUN WITH ME

Run with me under moonlit boughs
chasing our demons, nipping at lifted heels
while they race into the dark ahead, stars bursting
into constellations tracking the course of our love.

This love—why do they always call it love? when
the wolf in me lifts her head to howl with the moon,
it is *reverence.* when I lift my head to glare into your eyes
it is *defiance.* this is love   bursting into the air
where we will race beneath the ravens soaring.

Run with me, until we forget our human selves
until our skins shed away into the night and we no longer
need names beyond guttural sounds we christen each other,
we christen our bodies in love oils and hallowed sighs.

The scent of rosemary was in your hair, and *nag champa*
in your bones. *for remembrance,* I was told. But why does
the scent of my mother's head come to me in the night
silken waterfall strands I once clung to for dear life,
once calmed all the anxious storms of my child-mind.

Run with me, so we become untethered to the earth
and we don't recognize our reflections, head to toe
fur, eyes backlit moons in a sky of gray, white, amber
we are a pack, chosen family; run alongside me   and sing.

Epilogue: Fierce

My heart is open like a rose

but holds many thorns in place.

.:.

VOWS TO MYSELF

I vow to honor my Higher Self, to acknowledge that I am Deserving and Worthy, to Open to Expansion in my Life.

I vow to honor my emotions and my own expectations, to shed those of others/society which weigh me down.

I vow to love my body, to nourish and cherish it in every phase and form of its growth & metamorphosis. To honor mySelf in knowing I have a Choice in all I Become.

I vow to always hold my Soul in high regard, to listen deeply to what my intuition is speaking, and to live with full healing intentions for myself, and thus the greater world.

I vow to incarnate as my Inner Empress.

I vow to take my power in my hands and mold my life to that of my wildest dreams.

I vow to open myself to love, and being loved.

I vow to view myself as whole. I vow to honor my sacredness in all that she is, all that I am, and all that exists to fill and heal me.

HOW WOLVES AFFECT RIVERS

we've seen it in Yellowstone – trophic cascade;
the rush of river waters fell back from the bank –
where they once meandered, they became steady.
a rebirth of aspen, willow trees & cottonwood
the return of beavers, badgers and songbirds;
influx of bears (& berries), foxes & ravens,
even bald eagles came to feast on carrion –
an ecosystem brimming with regeneration,
all because of the Wolf.   (*keystone*)

SUMMONING THE WILD WOMAN

~ a mantra for the times we feel soul-lost

I Light a Beacon for my Wild Self to find her way back where she belongs. I call the name of my Higher Self and embrace back my Wild as she gradually returns.

I know I am both Wild thing Untamed and a Gentle Soul with an abundance of Love to offer.

I welcome Home my Wild Self from her soul travels, so she can heal and reintegrate within.

I know she will still run and play. I know she will have days when she becomes lost in the dark forest but together, we will forge a pathway home.

I welcome my Wild Woman; the parts of me that ache in ways I have no human language for - the parts of me forgotten and neglected, the parts of me that have been numbed and starved.

I beckon home all parts of my Self that make me who I am; usher them inside, make space for them, love them and my Wild Woman until I once again feel Whole and guided by the Divine.

Guru Jagat's Prayer

"May you not take no for an answer, question or statement.

Never talk about your weaknesses again as a way to dumb yourself down or become more relatable on social media or in a social construct.

Seriously discipline yourself to deeply care about your impact on everything that exists & seriously discipline yourself NOT TO CARE about what the spectators, critics, & pundits think, say, troll, & gossip about you.

May you breathe consciously and deeply even for a second longer today than yesterday and recognize what that means & what it does.

May the rising tides of pressure, Destiny & necessity continue to Wake you from the levels of dreaming, zombie life, status quo, & mind control — & allow the Sovereign Waking Dream reality to be bent, changed & challenged by your Conscious mind, body, heart & mission.

May the Punk Rock, Constant Questioner, Rebel with a Cause, immediate Intellectual, Community Organizer, GrassRooter, Boot Strapper, Warrior, Winner, Victor, Real Friend, Enlightened Leader, & Don't Stop til you Drop Ethos keep you."

An excerpt from WILDLANDS

NEW SKIN

stepping into that new skin I thought
might scar – felt like I could touch the whole
world swirled in the arch of my foot, that tender
sunrise-pink of regeneration. there is growth &
birth all around me –this morning I watched
as an eastern kingbird fetch bits of cut grass
dried then soaked through with rainwater
    we are boundless— everywhere we see
a creation of a new Universe; where we are
master, creator, goddess. claiming these new skins
as if we aren't imposters with stolen identities
already gazing at a foreign reflection wondering
which character we should portray today?
    is there an end to the seeking?
      the praying? the yearning?
        Or do we just
        let it all
        burn

MARSHLANDS

in the   marshlands
   where the wild has crept in &
      found solace in the clutch of
         knowing there is a place for

each & every creature...
   lily pads create a bridge
      for frogs & other amphibious beings

an ethereal crossway for dragonflies
   & Fairies   to enter our realm...

Acknowledgments & Inspirations

This collection and the poems herein are, like any book, born from a myriad of inspirations and created with a load of support and love. Thank you to all the tales (stories and books), legends and myths which offered fodder for creating this book of howls. ((Most of them are cited below but this is not an exhaustive list)).

To those who have been my blood, and my chosen pack, a wolf loves eternally. My husband, Scott, for not only accepting me in wolf-woman form (& actively encouraging me to howl), but also for truly seeing me; *jeg elsker dig*. Maya, my reader since I first started writing and built-in best friend since birth; the joy of watching you grow is unmatched, and seeing you become a nurse during the pandemic is full of courage I will admire forever. My mom, for being my infinite moonlight and constantly inspiring me to grow & shine. My dad, for always supporting my dreams. Jack'aroo' and my big bro Erik (+ Becca) for adopting me into your pack. My family in Denmark: Mum, Shell, Sars & Christel (plus Ronny and the doggies Nova and Dolly), for introducing me to hygge and loving me from day one. Renee & Jesse for showing me lasting friendship that's more like family. Rohan for being my soul friend. My MFA crew - 'Sexily Adverbing' for life - Vee, Charlie, Justin, Abi and Nicole. Shawna for the design inspiration & wolfy love. Everyone at Natural Lands, and to everyone who works for conservation of nature and endangered species.

And to everyone who has inspired me along the way - there are *countless* creative beings who express and share healing which gives me so much hope and joy; among them (in no particular order): Neel Trivedi, Maureen O'Dea, Mikey Carroll, L Sebastienne, Desi Monique (my beautiful mentor in sensual embodiment), Lisa Welsh (for helping me be 'Better in Bed'), Dr. Arielle Schwartz (who instructed me in Applied Polyvagal Theory in Therapeutic Yoga), Megan

Febuary ('For Women Who Roar'), and your insightful 'Dear Body December' prompts which created some of the poems herein, Sue Pierce (my lovely professor and Inside-Out mentor); and to Chris Sorrentino for being you, promoting me endlessly (and spending your last $15 on this book). S.B. for your edits on early versions of this poetry, and always being eager to read my work. B.L. for the breakthrough session that helped get me here. K.B. for your enduring love. You all keep me going and make the world a brighter place.

.:.

Some of these poems previously appeared in: *Ghost City Review, Elephants Never, Malarkey Books, Mookychick, Poetry in the Time of the Coronavirus* (print anthology, 2020), *Truly U Review,* among others. Thank you to the editors for giving them a loving first home.

A big special thank you and infinite gratitude to **Dr. Thema** for reading the following poems on her '**Homecoming**' podcast: *Love Yourself Wild* (from Prelude), featured on episode 100: 'Shifting a Trauma Mindset' (May 30, 2021); and *Vows to Myself* (from Epilogue), featured on episode 85: 'Eliminating Self-Destruction' (February 14, 2021).

Clarissa Pinkola Estés has kept me racing through the wilderness when I felt so very lost and hopeless. Her book became my Wild Woman Bible, full of infinite wisdom and the power of storytelling as a main source of inspiration (citation below). Thank you for such a gift to all women; for a solace I return to, often.

To everyone who sent me songs to help inspire, who gave words of encouragement, offered me love and friendship during even my darkest moments, *thank you*. You are so very loved, and I appreciate you more than words could ever express. And finally, to all those who live with the daily trials of complex PTSD and those who have endured any form of trauma: *may you continue to shine your light, and never dim it for anyone.*

.:.

Remember to support small, local bookstores!

Thank you to the following indie bookstores for stocking First Edition copies: **The Spiral Bookcase** (in-store: 4257 Main St., Philadelphia (Manayunk) and on-line: *thespiralbookcase.com*) and **The Head & The Hand** (2230 Frankford Ave., Philadelphia).

* * *

Citations

.:.

AFTERS

"Ginger Snaps", (pg. 34) – *after the movie: Ginger Snaps.* Directed by John Fawcett. Performances by Emily Perkins and Katharine Isabel. Motion International, 2000.

"Exsanguinate", (pg. 95) – *after the movie: Ginger Snaps 2: Unleashed.* Directed by Brett Sullivan. Performances by Emily Perkins, Tatiana Maslany and Katharine Isabel. Lionsgate Films, 2004.

"Sheila", (pg. 74) – *after the TV series: GLOW,* (aka *"Gorgeous Ladies of Wrestling"*), created by Liz Flahive and Carly Mensch, Netflix, 2017.

.:.

EPIGRAPHS, QUOTES & INSPIRATIONS

"body as an hourglass", (pg. 60) – Carson, Anne. "Totality: The Color of Eclipse." Cabinet Magazine, 2003, cabinetmagazine.org.

"La Loba", (pg. 47) *inspiration, and quotes* (pgs. ix, xv) – Estés, Clarissa Pinkola. *Women Who Run with the Wolves: Myths and Stories of the Wild Woman Archetype.* New York: Ballantine Books, 1992.

"Blood & Chocolate", (pg. 13) – *epigraph:* Hesse, Hermann. *Steppenwolf.* 19th edition, New York: Henry Holt and Company, 1963.

"How Wolves Affect Rivers", (pg. 137) – *inspired by:* "How Wolves Change Rivers." *YouTube,* uploaded by Sustainable Human, 13 Feb. 2014, www.youtube.com/watch?v=ysa5OBhXz-Q&ab_channel=SustainableHuman.

Epigraph (pg. xvii) – Jagat, Guru. *Invincible Living.* HarperOne, Illustrated Edition, 2017, print.

"Ode to the Wandering One", (pg. xiv) & *epigraph* (pg. 110) – Nin, Anaïs, and Gunther Stuhlmann. *The Journals of Anaïs Nin. Vol. 7: 1966-1974,* Owen, London, 1980.

"Singing through my Wolf Bones", (pg. 57) – *epigraph & inspired largely by:* Nuala Ní Dhomhnaill. "Abduction." ('Fuadach' in Irish). Translated by Michael Hartnett. *Selected Poems/Rogha Danta.* Raven Arts Press, Dublin, 1991.

Epigraph (pg. 51) – Plath, Sylvia. "Elm." *Sylvia Plath: Collected Poems*, Faber & Faber, 1981.

"*Wreckage*", (pg. 119) – epigraph: Rich, Adrienne. "Diving into the Wreck." *Diving into the Wreck: Poems 1971/1972*, Norton, New York, 2013. **Correction to First Printing:* "I came to explore the wreck."

"*Guru Jagat's Prayer*", (pg. 139); source: *ramayogainstitute.com*.

⁖

FOUND POEMS

Four (4) found poems in this collection are composed from words and phrases repurposed into poetry:

"*Lurid*", (pg. 103), and "*Kick a Hole in the Sky*", (pg. 127) – *found poem from:* Klause, Annette C. *Blood and Chocolate*. New York: Delacorte Press, 1997.

"*Lunation Ritual*", (pg. 8) – *inspired/adapted from text found in:* Konstantinos. *Werewolves: The Occult Truth*. Llewellyn Publications, September 2010.

"*Lessons in Being Human, Foreign*", (pg. 10) – *found poem from:* Russell, Karen. *St. Lucy's Home for Girls Raised by Wolves*. New York: Knopf, 2006.

⋰

MUSICAL MUSES

- a playlist

"*Hunger Swell*", part iii., (pg. 113) – Eilish, Billie. "All the Good Girls Go to Hell." *When We All Fall Asleep, Where Do We Go?*, Interscope Records, 2019, track 6.

"*You Flower/ Feast*", (pg. 6) – *inspired by:* Harry Styles. "Woman." *Harry Styles*, Columbia Records, 2017, track 9.

"*Blue Moon*", (pg. 29) – *inspired by:* Highly Suspect. "Wolf." *The Boy Who Died Wolf*, 300 Atlantic, 2016, track 11.

"*Cold as Steel*", (pg. 101), *epigraph & lyrics in italics:* Metallica. "Of Wolf and Man." *Metallica*, Elektra Records, 1991, track 9.

"*Wolf & I*", (pg. 53) – *title & emotions inspired by:* Oh Land. "Wolf and I." *Oh Land*, RCA Records, 2011, track 1.

"*Wolf Moon*", (pg. 70), *first line/italics are lyrics from:* TV on the Radio. "Wolf Like Me." *Return to Cookie Mountain*, Interscope Records, 2006, track 5.

In no particular order; these songs/artists helped me create: "Woman Who Runs with the Wolves" ～ Marya Stark; "She Wolf" ～ Shakira; Billie Eilish; FKA

Twigs; TV on the Radio; "MONTERO (Call Me By Your Name)" ~ Lil Nas X; "Black Leather" ~ Guns N' Roses; Wolfmother; "Run From Me" ~ Timber Timbre; and many more.

.:.

Check out my Spotify playlist (QR code above) "Singing through my Wolf Bones" for more musical inspirations. Happy Howling!

.:.

Dedicated with extra love to the **Wolves of Speedwell**, for inspiring me with your howls. Notably, Akela and Maka, Spirit and Mika, Yellow Feather and Loci... & to the **Ambassador Wolves** at Wolf Conservation Center; Nikai*, Alawa and Zephyr. A portion of all proceeds from this book will be donated toward wolf conservation efforts; Planned Parenthood; nonprofits benefitting SA survivors; and to Project HOPE (an international health care nonprofit aiding Ukrainian refugees & more; *projecthope.org*).

For further reading & more information on how you can help keep wolves (truly vital creatures) in existence:

Wolf Conservation Center, South Salem, NY, *nywolf.org*
* Nikai from *"Ode to the Wandering One"* is my symbolically adopted Ambassador Wolf.

Wolf Sanctuary of Pennsylvania, Lititz, PA, *wolfsanctuarypa.org*
(I began volunteer work here in March 2022.)

About the Poet: **Tianna G. Hansen** has been writing her whole life. She wanders woodlands as a wolf woman, howling at the moon in every phase. Tianna earned her MFA in Creative Writing: Fiction from Arcadia University in 2016, but poetry is her first love. She currently resides in Pennsylvania with her husband of 4 years (who she met in Edinburgh, Scotland - but he isn't Scottish!) and three cats: Stella 'Storm', her steady companion of 9 years (& nearly 9 lives!), plus newest additions from Berks Animal Rescue League: Tabby and Kismet aka "Kizzy", who were born with cerebellar hypoplasia. Much of her heart is at home in Denmark.

Find more of Tianna's work online at *creativetianna.com*, subscribe to her blog for updates or send her a howl at *creativet24@gmail.com* if you'd like to get in touch! Follow her on Instagram @embodiedhealingwithtianna or @goldencracked_words.

***

If you enjoyed this book, I would be so grateful for your thoughtful review on GoodReads, Amazon, or wherever you purchased it. Thank you for reading.